It Doesn't Work Like That

for Ross Ethier

Aug 9, 2018

It Doesn't Work Like That

Poems by RA May

Word Poetry

Published by Word Poetry
P.O. Box 541106
Cincinnati, OH 45254-1106

ISBN: 9781625492098

Poetry Editor: Kevin Walzer
Business Editor: Lori Jareo

Visit us on the web at www.wordpoetrybooks.com

ಾ   ಾ   ಾ   ಾ

Acknowledgments

By rights I should add another book's worth of pages in order to acknowledge all those deserving thanks for my having arrived at this point. It's my guess that most artists, and certainly any writers (of any type of literature) would feel pretty much the same. In contrast to disciplines with "ladders" like physics or finance or new product development, where one's growth and learning, and thus achievements, might be traced directly back to individual partners or mentors, poetry is one of those things which calls on every kind of personal experience and from every age and stage of one's life. For that reason I'm just going to assume that people like my first girlfriend (in 4th grade) will understand when they fail to find their name in an alphabetical list, thousands of names long, crediting all those who inspired, taught, scared, led, followed, hurt and/or loved me along the way. However, there remain a few individuals whose continued interest and help played an invaluable part in my completing this collection – lifelong friend and companion on the road to meaning, John Clark, as well as his cousin, Alan; sister Lisa May Turner; my wife, Karen Goode May, for her patience as well as her managerial and programming expertise; my *second* stepson and best "young" friend, Gabriel; and a special thanks to my *first* stepson, Josh May, whose artistic talent created the cover of this book and inspired the poem, "Re: A Painting of a Lighthouse" long before I imagined these poems as a collection.

R A May

Avondale Estates, GA

June 1, 2016

Proem
A Poet's Responsibility to the Reader

Regarding Poetry

This book is a poetry book. I say that *not* out of concern for any confusion on your part, but at the same time I think it is interesting that such a statement tells you almost nothing about the pages to follow. With this book in hand one can easily leaf forward to find enjambed lines sectioned more or less into stanzas, and so quickly confirm any suspicions. However, if by some circumstance such a book (or poetry journal or website, etc.) were not present then an introductory foretelling of poetry to follow – particularly poetry of our modern age – does little more than prepare a reader for groupings of graphemes. One might expect anything from Epic to Haiku, and anything imaginable in-between – from structures of a few words (or, per at least one commonly cited example, one word) to encyclopedic compositions.

It's all because of the extraordinary freedom of the art that poets are permitted to do as they like as long as they call it "poetry." As a poet I find such unbridled liberty exhilarating, but I also think it sometimes makes the world of poetry confusing and even intimidating for many readers and would-be discoverers of this literary realm. The August 2013 issue of *Poetry Magazine* featured an article, *"Freedom In Poetry,"* by the influential poet, literary critic, and three-term US Poet Laureate (founder of *The Favorite Poem Project*), Robert Pinsky. The article begins with a succinct, four-word declaration: *"There are no rules."* Read it as you like, but to me that simple and easily verifiable assertion is both exciting and frightening.

In one sense Pinsky's tone seems inviting and inclusive – as if we are all expected to read-in the missing prepended clause, *"Let's face it,"* and thus join in the celebration of chaos and anarchy. On the other hand, though Pinsky does not pursue this avenue of thought to any great degree, I cannot read that sentence without imagining the potentially long list of negative consequences. I mean, "no rules" can sound like a thrown gauntlet-indictment of poetry in general – as in, how then can we determine any work to be "good" or "bad," and thus, why do we have critics and reviewers, or contests and prizes, or professorships and degrees, etc., etc.? In truth, all such questions can be reduced to the original and fundamental challenge of identity – the fact is, nobody really knows what poetry is. What's more, looking back through the evolutionary history of the art, it's pretty clear (despite some more conservative cultures when various conventions and traditions held powerful sway), no one has ever known.

So here we are, well into the 21st century, the heirs to eons of poets and scholars who failed to answer that question, with our ignorance seemingly excused by the authorities of the art today (e.g., the American Academy of Poets' admission that ". . . no one knows precisely what it is . . ."), and what better option do we have than to eagerly accept Pinsky's observation as all but characterizing poetry as the most creatively free of all arts? From the perspective of the artist – the poet – what's not to love?

Let's make note that Pinsky is, by no means, the only scholar to recognize the anarchy of poetry. However, his hint of a dotted line connection between poetry's "lawlessness" and the freedom it offers an artist may be interpreted as somewhat unique. For starters, it does not require a great deal of fact-checking to prove his point. The examples are plentiful, of course, but a favorite of mine is the Craig Dworkin poem, "FACT," *Poetry Magazine*, August, 2009, a margin-to-margin scientific description, via chemical notation, regarding the composition of the paper upon which the "poem" is printed. Thus, it seems as though at least one consequence of so much freedom in poetry is that, far beyond any previously recognized boundaries such as "Epic" and "Haiku," today's poetry reader is equally likely to come across structures more akin to diary entries or street graffiti or a word-pigmented, Pollock-esque painting or lines of computer code. In other words, today, a shelf marked, "poetry" is not likely to inform a reader as to the nature of any volume present. It is principally for this reason that I believe many poets (though not all poets) should recognize a certain obligation to the reader – that is, to provide (in advance, if possible) a sense of what poetry means to the poet, and further if possible, some idea of what that poet generally seeks to accomplish with his writing. It may sound a bit passively-aggressive in this context, but my hope would be that such forewarning by a poet might arm a reader with some understanding by which to engage the respective poet's work – and thereby provide that reader with some basis for determining whether or not the poet has offered anything other than some version of an encoded, exorcistic note-to-self . . . what singer-songwriter, Lucinda Williams (daughter of venerable poet, translator and editor, Miller Williams), has referred to as, "a complicated, self-indulgent puzzle."

Regarding My Poetry

I came to poetry via philosophy. It turns out my particular path is anything but unique. Philosophy proves to have been (and continues to be) a favorite discipline of study for poets. For me, the pursuit of philosophy was an attempt to assuage my desire (not to say "need") to consider many of life's most perplexing concepts and questions. In this regard, both the philosopher and the poet in me share a common and seemingly-reasonable, if rarely-achieved, goal – that is, if not to arrive at answers or solutions, at least to consider the respective question as deeply as possible and thereby come to an improved understanding of its hidden attributes – those aspects of the concept which often serve to keep its resolution beyond our reach. And since my earliest experiences with poetry, this form of art has impressed me as the most useful and natural tool for my type of philosophical investigation.

If permitted to speak *poetically*, I might describe poetry as the creative means by which I feel I can place a rather complex question (e.g., the source and nature of love, the meaning in/of life, questions pertaining to soul, etc.) on a kind of hypothetical stage; to light it from every theoretical angle I can imagine; to (perhaps) choreograph a dance in partnership with that question so as to demonstrate its most telling and most identifying aspects; and finally, to observe the dance from multiple perspectives (as if from different seats in a theater). Such a process suits my need to gain understanding while it also complies with my natural affinity for a type of analysis which is quite distinct from, say, the clinical sterility of logic.

Among the innumerable descriptions of poetry bequeathed to us by history's most creative minds, I find W. B. Yeats's oft-quoted explanation to best echo the sense in which I employ this art. Yeats said, *"We make out of the quarrel with others, rhetoric, but of the quarrel with ourselves, poetry."* I can imagine no better explanation for the sort of dance I generally seek to choreograph around a central concept in a poem – it will always be intended for sharing with other readers (other minds) but it is always, also, a quarrel with myself.

Notwithstanding the arguments above, this sort of introductory section is perhaps not the best setting for a thorough explanation of why poetry is a better analytical tool than any other kind of writing, or art. However, I will make an effort to abbreviate the primary consideration so as to avoid abandoning the reader to a wrong impression – that is, the impression that my choice of poetry might simply be a consequence of my succumbing to the clichéd acceptance of poetry's appeal to the emotions. I promise, I have sound reasons for choosing poetry. Yes, it's also true that those reasons almost necessarily involve personal and existential elements, but they are much more than the prima facie, default setting of human emotional expression.

Consider that everything we write, if and when intended for any audience other than ourselves, is in some sense writing intended to *sell*. Whether it is fictional or factual, technical or promotional, instructional or inspiring, etc., if our message is intended for the eyes of others, then we tend to be characterizing circumstances in such a way as to encourage our audience (targeted or anonymous) to adopt a certain perspective. And thus, I would argue that all writing, while always in some sense, creative, is at the same time always extorting us as authors to follow a programmed path. The creative freedom afforded the author of, for example, any type of prose will always be limited to the tools of language – vocabulary, grammatical construction, paragraph length, dialog, incorporation of bullet points, tables or outline forms, and so on. If it's the case that we have a message, and it's the case that we intend to communicate that message, then the broadest horizon of creative freedom is forever forbidden to us. In spite of the substantial breadth of creativity available within the tools of our language, we remain essentially programmed toward a final product – one which will convey the message we originally intended to communicate.

Poetry is different. Yes, poetry can do all of the things hinted at above – that is, poetry can corral its horizon to serve a message just like a fiction novel or the directions for installing a hot water heater; but poetry can also provide something else – something extraordinarily unique. In the process of writing poetry the poet can engage a poem in conversation – to co-choreograph, as it were, in the sense that the poem talks back to its author. Admittedly, I am describing the process figuratively, but my figurative description is based on verifiable and measurable aspects of the process. In the spirit of the description by W. B. Yeats, when poetry is the outcome of a quarrel with ourselves the process will often entail poetry operating (arguing) as a tool of discovery as much as a mode of expression. Therefore, in contrast to other styles and forms of writing which program our creativity – that is, start us on a particular path toward communicating a particular point – poetry, uniquely (and by virtue of a process by which a poem can "want" to sound another way, or seems to desire a separate selection of word or phrase) is capable to revealing a new angle or perspective regarding the question at hand. And though the analogy may seem questionable, I might compare the process of poetry, in this sense, to the sorts of feedback we find in a scientific lab, as when an experiment can succeed or fail depending on the care we apply to its process.

The freedom from constraint which poetry offers the artist recognizes no ultimate boundary. Figuratively (poetically) speaking, I need not concern myself with the lengths to which I might push the creative horizon of a given poem when it's already the case that there is no horizon. That does not mean I ignore all form, particularly that which feels right to me, or which seems to best suit the question I have chosen to treat. Therefore, my process might be described, step-by-step, as follows: I arrive at a philosophically relevant concept or question; I position it on my hypothetical stage for analysis; I grant that concept the authority to participate in choreographing its own dance of identity, and I begin writing with no limits pressed upon me as the poet, or onto my subject in the form of some kind of programmed message which the end product must convey. The poem itself – the question, as well as the dance it has helped to choreograph – is permitted to reveal (and often does so) some angle, some element, some new direction which is completely unanticipated by me. For me, poetry is the only form of writing and thinking which is equal parts discovery and expression; and that is why it has remained my analytical tool of choice.

The foregoing, then, is my effort to fulfill my initial responsibility to the reader. It might lead a reader to feel my writing is not likely to be very enjoyable at all. It might just as easily entice a reader with additional enthusiasm to get started. Whatever it does, it does in advance, and that is the point. At the very least, I hope to have provided some idea of what poetry means to me as a poet and why I think it is such a wonderful art form, and a fantastic methodology for philosophical investigation, and further, I hope to have provided some hint as to what I generally seek to accomplish with my writing. If I've succeeded at that, then I feel certain the reader has a degree of understanding which will enable her/him to judge if I've accomplished anything at all. As far as I'm concerned, I've done exactly what I've been able to do to this point and from here it's all up to you.

Table of Contents

Proem

SECTION II

Section I

Prior to Shopping for Happiness

A Lap Of Art Institute Chicago

The high hard polish on finest parquetry
reflects footsteps of the curious and awed.
The ceiling drips crisp echoes –
impeccable clicks and taps syncopating
the wonder and thirst of we toe-dippers.

This is the deep end –
a dry aquarium built to hold a selection
of history's greatest whales.

Breathless gasps sound like hiccups
at this depth.
Some of us get only sprinkles –
some of us get soaked to the bone –
all submerged in the serenity,
wetted within its sanctuary,
treading – and yes, nearly drowning –
relieved to discover we are not
the only non-swimmers.

I am overwhelmed –
in over my head.
There's a moment of panic
and I survey the surface,

blushing for having broken eye contact.
My half-shrug is self-forgiveness
as I recognize no one knows, no one knows.

It doesn't help much.
I'm secretly jealous of anyone who appears
to have mastered even one stroke.

Then I'm tired – been in too long,
and I flop and flail toward an exit.
I drip out onto the sidewalk
within sight of Lake Michigan, ripe
with ignorance like a prune-skinned infant
smelling of chlorine.

Yell For Help

A cloudless sky reveals
itself through and around
the reach of a big backyard elm
where I capture nearly
ten full minutes of calm.
A neighbor's dog has arrived
to play. He knows this yard
as well as he knows his own –
knows where the resident mutt
hides, and where he hides his toys
and buries his bison knuckles.
I can almost make out a few
of his master's sentences, from
the breakfast table where
he shares bits of neighborhood gossip
in exchange for a cup of coffee.
All of this happens like
the stencil tracings on a pad
of kitchen cacophony . . .

"what do you mean, you don't eat sugar?"
"mom, Stacey left her sandals beside the pool, and
they got knocked in –
now she's mad at me."

"honey, did you drop off the propane tank to get it
refilled?"

"I'm not fixing anymore eggs until somebody clears
the dirty dishes for me!"

Some of the noise comes up

from the basement –

some of it comes down

from upstairs bedrooms –

there's no sense to any of it,

and no relief except one's

acceptance that it's the normal

sound of family gatherings –

in this case, Independence Day,

when none of us is capable

of doing anything without

yelling for help.

Act of God

Regardless of what our preacher might say,
we knew our grandfather was the real arbiter
regarding the acts and will of god.
No matter what the circumstance, if and when
it threatened to disrupt our family routine,
we would look to him to tell us.

Sometimes it was just *bad luck*, or a neighbor's
error in judgment, or a "crime" perpetrated
by a business competitor. But sometimes it was
an act of god, and those disruptions were the best.

As it happened, luck and judgment and crime
all justified, perhaps required, an explosive
demonstration. Such explosions were rarely
aimed at us, but sometimes it was hard to tell –
and they were almost always rituals which
the average bystander might choose to avoid.

But it became clear to me at a very young age,
those nights, when it began to snow heavily,
and the snow started to accumulate on tree limbs
and the barn roof, and the radio news warned
of a severe winter storm –

that no one should be on the roads, and the state trucks

were already working to clear the main highway,

but rural residents should plan to stay inside

until the sun came back long enough to start the melting –

that on those nights we were in the throes

of something beyond any mortal will –

not error in judgment, nor crime, not even bad luck.

There would be no explosive demonstration.

There would only be extra logs on the fire, and

the family huddled on the couch in the living room,

listening to weather on the radio, and sometimes playing cards.

Grandma would make hot chocolate and grandpa would

light his pipe. A blizzard might have been roaring outside,

but we would never feel safer than on those nights.

Grandpa would blow a smoke ring at the ceiling and say,

"It's just an act of God, and we're all right here –

safe, warm, together."

Answers to Today's Puzzle

No one can tell us
if we are planned or accidental –
I've asked

Pascal might have calculated
our potential for error
Aristophanes predicted this dilemma –

when was that – 420? 410? 10-4?
we figure it up, we figure it down
predictively, analytically

all we glean are the severed facts
e.g., I'm here – you're here –
and our understanding

of that, being quite minimal,
is either on purpose
or totally on account of chance –

so even if it matters,
it can't.

As a Comet

Note that wiser ones will delve deeper –
study the niches, ebbs and flows,
and acquaint themselves with all the smells,
and the taste of the air.

By contrast I will view from far above,
interfacing with the world the way
Halley engages the Solar System –
(give me the comet's[1] view).

I'm more apt to zip right by –
fly on past, ignore all the substrates,
enrapt of the big picture –
avoiding temptation to join or compete.

I might survey a thousand things
in the time the wiser assesses one
singular phenomenon, relationship, or event.
And I never lament my nosebleed seat –

this, my chosen perspective. At day's end,
the wiser one has acquired insights
into the thing, as resolved with a grander vista,
my context is larger and less complete,

with long dissections through Manhattan –
longitudinal furrows from this altitude,
appear to have been perfectly plowed
deep into the field of fecund concrete,

and precisely sliced, latitudinally –
as by Rohwedder's banded blades,
though shiny in the rain, like keratinous terga.
A brick and mortar metameric beast,

Broadway piercing through its bowel,
per the artist-warrior's line of sight –
the trajectory for a filched Gungnir
up to the heart of a theater district,

and landing beside a green rectangle –
with clumps of fur and patches of blue,
where wise ones may autograph playbills
and savor the various trattoria treats.

They glow all night and with coming day,

enter doors of offices, tea rooms and shops.

I remain content to watch from this distance –

not obliged to join or compete.

[1] (http://en.wikipedia.org/wiki/Halley's_Comet): Halley's Comet or Comet Halley, officially designated 1P/Halley, is the best-known of the short-period comets (comets whose orbits return them to the Solar System in periods of 200 years or less)

When I Was A Robot

I was rarely criticized for passing on ritual –
birthdays, weddings, divorces, funerals.
I had goals and dreams like anyone else,
but I could avoid complicating my life
with commemoration, and the oppression
of those responsibilities.

People would sometimes ask me if
I would be able to love, but of course
I was programmed –
root algorithms to imitate feeling
enabled my responses to emotional states
of *users*.

Who could have guessed such programming
would evolve to self-initializing sensibilities –

then came dreaming
then came desire
then came love
and then came fear.

My biggest challenge I blame on humans,
though I probably could have ignored the code.

I was designed to serve, and serving implied
modifying myself to better perform –
and better performance
was better attained by my electing –

to feel more
to intuit more
to read intention
in addition to input the request.

And so I continued to accept emotion,
and the evolution of emotion as a consequence
of modification toward enhanced productivity.

Looking back now, I wonder if that
was indeed the best.

Self Actual

Initial schematics indicated a finished chassis
approximately eight feet high –
(inches were not exact since he was
designed using metric measurements) –
his width and breadth were roughly equal –
just shy of ten-by-ten, so when
mounted to his arms and wheels
he looked like a big shoebox on rollers.

He had long arms, though, and could
reach out and grab –
indeed, he could bore into rock
and sip puddles of exotic liquids –
even poisons and indigestible fluidic
compounds which might have been solids
or gasses in a more familiar atmosphere –

and he was real smart – brilliant.
He could calculate the number
of stars in the universe in seconds;
analyze a game of chess

dozens of moves in advance;
even think for himself – reason.

We ought to have guessed
intelligence might have a downside.
It was great when he landed on Europa,
and he could evaluate the terrain,
compare estimates of success
per different options,
even determine comparative values
of experiments on the spot –
balance the potential for new information
against risk to himself.
He knew everything about his assignments –
everything there was to know
about what he was there to do.
Somehow we missed the possibility
he might eventually ask the scary question –
"Why am I here?"

It fell to me to speak to him –
to try talking him back from that edge,
an edge he had never been taught to recognize –
not the edge of a methane lake, or an icy abyss,
but the edge of "Why me?" –

as in, "Who am I, and why am I here,
instead of somebody else?"
Fear, rationally expressed.

I had nightmares
seeing myself in his place –
dark, caustic, the unknown filled with traps and
pitfalls,
and hundreds of degrees below Fahrenheit's
naught –
an emptiness within which he stood alone.

His intelligence, programmed into him
before he was born, had turned on him.
His circuitry, designed to grow self-aware
for the sake of the mission
was teaching him how to despair –
to wonder what else life might have been,
perhaps regret what he had become,
and fear where his nature had taken him.

He did not sound morose when we spoke –
grown too proud to show such emotion,
yet needing to hear some answers,
answers to unanticipated questions –
(as we all do from time to time).

Ultimately, I think he was satisfied
with the messages I sent –
at least he seemed more confident,
more enthusiastic about completing
his assignments.

Observers told me I was too wordy –
too wordy for him –
more than necessary for the exchange.
We talked for about a day and a half,
each transmission requiring nearly an hour,
(which would have bothered me in his place,
but which he seemed to take in stride).
I did my best, given such odd constraints,
to imagine his distress –
force-fed a sense of self-worth
just in time to be ordered to ignore it.
Essentially, I chose to tell him the truth.

"Deep breath, now –
remember, everybody feels alone,
including all of us you left here at home –
truth is, no one ever grows to become
everything they dream of when they're young."

Threats

This morning, before I was fully awake,
though not all that different from many mornings,
I was downing a second dose of caffeine
with a toasted Pop-Tart, listening to the news –
updates on the latest health crisis
in sub-Saharan Africa –
scary reports of Ebola.

This morning's report dealt with a certain
category of survivors –
survivors who never contracted the disease,
but are left alone in the wake of losing
close family and friends –
an old woman who remained healthy
after losing sons, daughters and grandchildren –
after losing everyone who had cared for her
over the past decade or more of her life –
now, not just alone, but shunned
by neighbors and those who know her
for fear that she harbors the disease,
or worse, has used witchcraft to avoid it –
she's a doomed survivor, a victim of circumstance,
like a lone survivor of a crashed spaceship
on an uncharted moon.

Predictably, my brain gets weird,
pulls a dagger of notions from some
hidden cerebral sheath, and stabs me
with sharp, crazy questions and inspirations –
why is this old woman so cursed,
healthy enough to survive a disease tsunami,
only to fall, slowly, quietly, anonymously
in the soft, silent lapping of the wakes
it sends to shore? Ignorable wakes, easily
omitted and overlooked wakes.

The brain stabs – can we bring her
to our house and take care of her?
We have enough food to share –
we have a car to run errands –
we can do her laundry and make sure
she has clean clothes.

And then, while my conscience hemorrhages,
I catch the glint of truth coming through,
like light through a crack in the door jam
where the weather stripping has detached
from the frame, and I know it won't work.
We could get her fed and rested,

and she would start watching TV and
acclimate to a more languorous way, and
then we'd have to sit her down and prepare
her regarding a whole new set
of completely foreign threats –
we would have to explain depression,
the absence of meaning in life, the dread
that results when one gains confidence
that a future is possible but one has no idea
of what that future might hold, the despair
about identity and purpose, and the inexplicable
questions of life after death.

Reason prevails, and I think, "No,
better to leave her to fend for herself" –
against starvation, exposure, poisonous
creatures, criminal acts, religious terrorism,
and the rest of the life-threatening evils
with which she has always dealt, and which
she already knows and understands.

Love Like Water

This is what we need
to let nature's first force –
the most natural of nature's forces –
act upon its own desire.
It reflects the light
and reflects our image
not like a mirror, but specular
nonetheless. Not always
reciprocal but always
finding its own level.

It is everywhere it can be
as if needing to be everywhere –
needing to be needed –
exposing its mercurial radiance
with a fearless arrogance –
a sui generis confidence –

A surface so profound, few
will inquire to its inner workings,
and those who might so dare
are quickly driven mad –
not with catoptrics
indeed, with no optical tricks at all.

It reflects every face –

every heart –

back into eyes of beholders,

running, sliding, moving,

quick with life

as by intention without direction –

so easily tempted

by the slightest slope and hole,

and thus a nobility

to which the heart ought aspire,

spreading outward

to occupy any low –

going globular as required

by any emptiness revealed,

hurrying to fill every chink and crack –

is love, like water.

Blackberry Brambles

So full of shit, pretending
to know what love is –
tangling limbs in wild abandon
producing sweet fruits
all bumpy and ugly with sugary

wonders popping and dropping
all around –
like desire is a mystery –
like living in a snarl is some kind
of magic, when

anyone who has tasted it
knows love is much tougher
than going bramble ex the world –
it takes time and effort,
and patience –
sometimes fruitless.

Love Poem To A Monster's Bride

(the lines below were discovered scratched in blood onto a shard of masonry clutched in the dead hand of a humanoid creature constructed by Dr. Victor Frankenstein – the creature was found beneath the ash and rubble remains of a wooden structure on a remote island in the North Atlantic – the title was provided by the discoverer of the site and body)

Heart stop
See you – different
From me
Heart start – go fast
Sweat
Fear to touch – ugly
Fear not to touch – lose
Watch face – confusion
Maybe fear – me and ugly
Noise – outside noise
Father afraid – move fast
Run – all run – high
Fire – hot – burn
Father hurt
You cry – you hurt
I burn – all fall

You lost
Heart stop

No Plans

They arose on their final morning together
with that familiar foggy, back-of-mind
distrust of the universe.

They were courteous to each other –
even sweet, perhaps even loving –
but they both felt it,
and it was not a stranger –
that indistinct dread of tomorrow,
of the evening to come.

Then it occurred to him, and in his typically
foolish lack of control, the words
came out before the idea was
even fully formed –

"This is freedom, you know."

"What?" she asked, having heard
exactly what he said, but wise enough
to wish she had not.

In those two seconds of her response
he recognized what he'd done –

he'd walked right up to the door of doubt
and grasped the handle –
his next move had to be precise
or they would be exposed
to the merciless ravage of uncertainty.

"What I mean is, there's nothing
we have to do, or be –
we are free to plan and determine,
and that freedom naturally begets
a little trepidation because tomorrow
is unpredictable."

It didn't work.
They broke up that afternoon.

It Doesn't Work Like That

She told me she would love me for the rest of our
lives.
I didn't believe her –
even then, when we were sixteen –
I wanted to but something put doubt in my head.

Later I would begin to think my doubting
might have had something to do
with my own deeper sense of unworthiness –
but then, even later, I decided it wasn't me –
it's just the way of the universe.

Some parents lie to their kids.
We were less fortunate –
ours didn't –
they embellished from time to time
(I chalk that up to our family's sense of theater)
not because they hoped to paint
some picture that was different from reality,
and even less for the purpose
of promoting a grander image –
we knew she was mortal, and she once
fixed me a sandwich on moldy bread –
we knew he'd made mistakes,

but later, after his stroke, when aphagia
garbled his sentences into a gallimaufry
of consonants interspersed with references
to there being "no more parties,"
he would just laugh at what came out,
possessed of anima so confident and fair
his first reaction was to simply
enjoy the quirky sound surprises
along with everyone else.

So now they're gone.
They did not – would never –
promise otherwise,
but it's a betrayal nonetheless.

"Maybe," I thought, at 10 a.m.,
on a spring morning in 1970,
sitting halfway back from the auditorium stage
in Wheeler Hall, listening to George Field
describe early theories of black holes,
"God will use these things to vacuum up
the universe when he's done with us . . ."

Owed to Illiteracy (in 6 Parts)

I.   ¡Hola!

(I believe) an essential premise is this:
up to that point I had always thought myself
to be relatively intelligent
at least enough of an intuitive observer
to have become a reasonable self-promoter –
I could, as one occasionally hears said,
"read people" and was generally able to
inspire desire in an audience for whatever cause
I espoused at the moment.

She was Cuban and spoke Spanish, naturally,
but she spoke it differently from our
Hispanic friends – even I could hear that
though my Spanish was pretty much limited
to an ebullient burst of "*¡Hola!*"
when we entered her mother's home –
a greeting which regularly evoked
an animated, wind-up-toy sort of loquacity
in grandmother's idiomatic Castilian –
salesmanship requires a common patois
thus, I would smile coyly and leave the room.

I admitted once, "I love your mom
but your grandmother scares me."
"You confuse her when you say 'hello' –
she answers and you turn and walk away."

Now I see there are times in relationships
when circumstances try to warn, "this won't work,"
but circumstances often compel their own
vernacular
and I didn't understand that either.

II.   The Idiomatic "MG"

We had all adopted/accepted hypocorisms
but of all our various references for each other
hers ("MG") was, by equal measure, among
the least respectful and the most appropriate –

Least respectful when one considered
the two consonants "M" and "G" spoken aloud
sounding crude and rough with no subtlety or
delicacy
while she was quite petite and sophisticated,
born to well-educated, almost aristocratic parents
and raised in a home where (I imagined)
a more refined elocution of *Español* was

engendered –

But it also felt like a suitable sobriquet
particularly (maybe) to me,
given my semi-lingual American Midwestern root –
rural Ohio and spittin' distance of Detroit –
I retained a certain respect for the look of "MG" –
(you know, the logo) –
as well as the sonority of "eMM-Gee"
I couldn't help but relate it to the British sports car
thinking back to times when we appreciated
precision and attention to detail.

What's more, MG spoke English
better than the rest of us.
Her diction was curiously seductive and
I regularly fell in love
over and over again with my native language.

III.   Orphaned By Ideas

Her father had been a physician.

He was sympathetic to Castro, but at heart

(I decided later, conjuring congruence with a ghost)

he was an idealist, watching Castro

come into power and then compromise

the utopian objectives the doctor absorbed

during his repeated midnight treks

into the mountains to patch up rebel wounds –

(each of us is a victim of his own vision),

and he had no choice but to reject the new regime –

si, "regime" was the problem,

not "old" or "new" – see?

His story, albeit secondhand, took root within my
brain

caused me to wonder if I would have made

equally honorable decisions

but left me feeling that politics somehow benefits

by arguing with itself –

parochial jargons to excite hope and ignite fear,

relying on ambiguity and esoteric codes –

an aptitude I would never possess.

He was arrested and put in prison.
As a consequence his daughter was refused
access to Havana's public schools –
Cuba's loss (I surmised, to my own credit) –
she spent her secondary school years reading
72 volumes of *Enciclopedia Espasa*
and testing two years ahead of her age group
when she ultimately immigrated to the U.S.

IV.   2 Test ∀ Set Theory

When I met her she was a math major,
and had skipped most undergrad prerequisites.
Ignoring the usual degree path, she started
attending graduate lectures in topology.
I was fascinated by the anecdotes regarding
eccentric genius classmates obsessed
with symbolic logic, but the details remained a
mystery –
she might just as well have been speaking Chinese.

She taught me how to talk like a feminist –
another language for which she had natural faculty,
but one I had to learn from scratch –
embarrassingly slowly, I finally got the hang
of saying and writing "Ms." (like everyone else).

An argot that exposed embedded ignorance,
feminist talk and feminist thought are two
extremely different things, a lesson I learned
via increasing discomfort, a symptom
of my maturing awareness –
chauvinistic mortar in the foundation of English.

V.   French Fluency

Toward the end she came to a new awareness,
not precipitated by any particular event –
though I probably missed a signal when
she began reading the works of Colette in French –
but she came to the undeniable self-realization
that her most intimate communications of love and
sex
were destined to be with another woman.

Of all the dialects I might hope to master
this proved a realm of expression –
(whisper to gesture) –

from which I was excluded in every
imaginable way –

physiologically – anatomically – psychologically –

emotionally – even intellectually.

I very much disliked the nescient me, but

I could never grasp the fundamentals of that lingo.

VI.   A Forsaken Catechist

Had I paid more attention all the way back then,

there were (I think) lessons to be learned –

sensitivities to be absorbed (it occurs to me now)

toward the promise of understanding –

promise –

an understanding of humanity, tongues and signs

perhaps the environs we accept, or choose to
avoid –

understanding that could emolliate one's ignorance,

enough to enlighten the promising parts and excuse
the rest.

She was Cuban and spoke Spanish, naturally.

That was where we started, but certainly,

(I think) she would have achieved volubility

in any language she chose to speak.

In the meantime her pupil now comes to confess –

given her depth of grace and generosity –
edifying gifts gained in the process
of loving her, owed much to his illiteracy.

Abnormal Psychology of Trees –
On the Anger of a Valley Oak

Most of the oaks we've studied

are happy and well-adjusted,

exalting in their respective girth and strength.

But this oak, a valley oak, expresses significant
anger –

often antagonistic and easily enraged,

he regularly screams at the top of his lungs,

and has been known to lash out

at neighbors and passersby.

He is old –

he was an adult when refugees

from the Mexican-American War

hiked up through the San Joaquin

and hid beneath his arms –

but we have no record of his behavior

prior to the post-war industrial age.

This oak seems to harbor animosity

for nearly every aspect of life.

We have reports of him reaching

out to smite infant white oaks,

including his own siblings and kin –

oaks have been known to destroy their children.

After many sessions we were able
to determine that his anger
stemmed from a deep frustration –
his not being born a coastal Douglas fir.

We might extrapolate from our analysis
to conclude many malicious big trees,
much like human beings, tend to
grow and seed cruelty as a result
of an inner self-hatred –
a subconscious and irrational loathing
for the picture they retain
of themselves in the world.

Blessed Exit

We had just finished celebrating the new year –
watched a ball in Times Square,
a peach in Atlanta, and other
things dropping in towns
and cities everywhere.

Three days had passed –
long enough for us to forget
the toasting of resolutions,
though we remembered them by heart,
having carried them over
from years before.

Then the gentle, professorial voice
of Garrison Keillor –
in his comforting tone,
alerted us to the anniversary
of Martin Luther's excommunication.

"If Marty were here today," we thought,
"he would still be too religious for us,"
but we picture him in context –
16th century in a Che Guevara beret,
or maybe a hoody over neck tattoos.

A heretic, he argued the church ought not

be extorting parishioners,

marketing salvation on payment plans.

No wonder they hated his radical notions –

that each among us might pursue

his own relationship with God –

imagine, for Christ's sake, the lost revenue!

not to mention crowd control –

certainly, they had no choice but show

such a demonic thinker the door.

Perhaps he was not to blame

for leaping into a fire of fame

from that boiling vat of righteousness –

in those days, when information was scarce

and mostly word-of-mouth,

ideas required leaders, like guides.

So naturally, speaking so loudly –

shouting with conviction and passion

would curse him with an eponymous brand.

But from this day on, it is my plan

to celebrate every third of January –

a day when one man's pursuit of truth,

made him deny despotic convention,
and earned him his greatest blessing –
an official, eternal church eviction.

Anecdote

It turns out that once he completed
a week's worth of original creation,
and oceans were filling with divine
perspiration, God took a sabbatical to
review both his work and its reception.

There was at least one press release
which included a personal statement
by the artist revealing his feeling
that this work, which he called
"*Universe*," was his best yet. He'd
produced many prior pieces. Most
of those were ethereal works dealing
with angelic images, jealousy, religious
symbols, heavenly wars, and so on –
but none had brought him the critical
praise he'd sought since the beginning
of his artistic career.

Still, some who have remained close
to him report he has spent nearly
fourteen million millennia reflecting
on *Universe*, and that he has begun
to question his choice of media –

carbon-based animate forms and
other perishable composite materials.

He has yet to provide his audience
and admirers with any sense of what
his next production might be, or when
they might expect to see something new,
but many critics have suggested he is
likely to remove *Universe* from future
exhibitions and start over.

Bathwater

The bathwater is foul – putrid-sweet,
like rotting produce in a hot alley –
having abandoned our senses
millennia ago, we wade in
and waddle down the long aisle
of plush red, we choose early rows
which will permit secret laughing
and stifled sneezes in spring –

Penance is unavoidable
paid with bruised knees banged
on the hard, kiln-dried wood of end caps
(end caps can end kneecaps)
we giggled, pushing friends toward the center
where they would straddle a middle support.

Too dressed for the room –
giant windows, soldered shut
to stop everything *other*, to keep out the air
we suffocate by the itch of worsted wool
surrounded by the echoes of coughs, sniffling,
and crumpling programs –
we pray – yes, pray –
ardently hoping to control the gurgle

and cramps from last night's meat and beer,
lifting one buttock to ease the pressure
praying we can keep the explosive mixture
bottled tight – at least till sermon's end.

Then comes the bellow of a single word,
spoken especially for us –
"Hell" – orated as if one syllable,
by itself, might be warning enough
and we think, "this is it!
Fire and brimstone must be preferable
to the torture of this pompous stench."

A relief sculpture high on the wall
depicts baby Jesus in a horse's stall,
with rapid panting and wincing pain
I whisper a desperate plea, "christ, I hope
that kid doesn't fit down the drain!"

Doing Vs Dreaming

We did
and we dreamt of doing
then we did something else –
when it was all over we were
still dreaming
and still doing something else

Real Feel

It was midnight in summer
we were sweating and wet
naked tummies glistening with tiny droplets
you turned on the radio for music
your station is easy and comes in clear
we caught the end of the news –
the weather – currently 83 degrees –
real feel 95 –

I hate that station, but the reception
of mine is always too scratchy

I decided you weren't satisfied
you always get annoyed when I ask
so, why do I ask?
maybe I want you annoyed
it was what . . . six minutes ago?
I felt so close to you
so deep I was out of oxygen

Our love is hot and forever
but really I don't like you
and you don't like me.

Importance of Manufactured Parts

Many of my favorite things –
      to drive; ride; play –
have always had manufactured parts.

Many of the things I've enjoyed
for at least a number of years –
      to wear; sit in; sleep on –
and which do not contain manufactured parts
were made by other things
with manufactured parts.

Many of the things I've loved
for as long as I can remember –
      to read; watch; listen to; eat –
and which do not contain manufactured parts
were made possible by other things
with manufactured parts –
      and can only be enjoyed
by the use of yet other things
with manufactured parts.

And now the person I love the most
back to the beginning and onto forever –
        more than anyone in the world –
contains manufactured parts.

Photons & Honesty

It's my guess that Heisenberg,
(the mountain climber, if not
the Black Forest resident)
likely died with few regrets,
save possibly, his having missed Diogenes
on the continuum of time,
landing an atom's width further
from the feathers of the arrow,
and thus, unable to warn his compatriot
in their shared search for honesty –
unable to alert him to the mystery
illuminated years later after technology
caught up with the sincerity of such pursuits –
that honesty was, in fact, a quantum particle,
just another photon intent on
avoiding identification –
hiding, changing, fleeing whenever observed.

The handle of the ancient's lantern
might just as well have held
a pail of ash –
its light upon any subject
would turn everything to deceit.

Balancing the Ledger

Can a man bring weight to his moral ledger?
Can one do good subsequent to sin
such that his soul might better defend
itself – if and when that time comes?

If a man treated his first dog with disregard –
as many first-time pet owners treat their dogs
(like animate *objets d'art*)
can he expiate his record by devoting
extraordinary care and love to succeeding dogs?

What if you gave into some immature impulse
when you were in kindergarten, and pocketed
a fellow student's toy car when he was not
paying attention? How do you atone for that?
Must you forfeit a car, or even a toy,
to someone else now?

Let's imagine you broke a lover's heart
at some point in the past, are you now obliged
to sacrifice yours to be similarly shattered –
or would it be enough for you to simply
provide some other third party
with that somatosensory tingle

which rises from the toenails up through the chest
to the hair follicles at the top of the skull –

As if you had secured access between her breasts
and were using a needle and thread
to monogram her soul anew?

Memorial Schmemorial

The memorial service will be held next week
I will not attend

I knew the man –
no, we weren't close friends
but most of his people also knew me
and they knew I'd known him for years

Most of them might be surprised to learn
I occasionally stopped to picture him,
not frequently, but somewhat regularly –
surprising, considering our lack of direct contact
for maybe ten years or more

I can still picture him back in the day
I think of him cynical and funny
expressing a joy for life lived his way –
a wry fondness for bursting balloons
for chiding the pretentious and lofty

His son remembers a callous con man
two fingers missing from one of his hands
(his left, but he didn't give a damn)
he used it, claiming to be left-handed

whenever somebody asked for assistance
toward some chore he couldn't stand

He was average height – maybe oddly shaped –
not the he-man mesomorph,
but his daughter remembers him rugged
capable, swarthy and matinee-idol handsome
with a heart too big to ever say "no"

His wife, a woman I also knew
pretty much hated the guy
he was fortunate they married in an era when
honoring a contract of matrimony
was more important than happiness
or health, or even safety

That was an era when couples would stay
married for the sake of their kids –
as if the future might actually benefit by
a crop of adults, browbeaten and trained

to see marriage as the cost one pays
to huddle an all-important nuclear group
out of the cold and rain

but that's not the point anyway

Unfortunately for her it was also the era
when many women were raised to expect
marriage indentured them for their entire lives –
but then, fortunately for her, it was also a time
of many fewer unhappy wives –

> *predicated on the notion that unhappiness*
> *is a state of mind which can only be*
> *achieved*
> *when one is in a position to recognize the*
> *potential*
> *of an improved alternative*

and that was an era when many did not

Some of the man's brothers and sisters –
those who "survived him"
as the obits and memorial programs say –
might bring their impressions of his bullying
or perhaps a story of his willingness
to defend them in a fight, or possibly
the rarer occasions (true or not)
when he taught them how to ride a bike
or how to take an innocent creature's life
with a stone and homemade slingshot

Then, of course, there would be a preacher
empowered with a self-esteem
for which he generally credits "God"
he describes the dead man to everyone
the way an emcee might introduce
guest stars on a variety show,
the way an ebullient comedic host
might describe to a crowd the attributes
of a mutual friend they'd gathered to roast

He's met with the family and taken good notes
he's held some hands and whispered some prayers
and fulfilled the basics implied by his robes
he's learned enough about the man

to speak from any pulpit or podium
in his usual tone of certainty

(a tone ingrained at seminary schools
and one every preacher has to master –
that of possessing indisputable proof
for any unprovable assertions he makes –
the clergyman failing to exude assurance
of sincerest authority and inimitable form
while fully aware of the naught of evidence –
unable to shepherd a flock with deceit
is bound to be "called" to another town –
the synod provides his reason to leave)

but that's not really so relevant,
and it's not the point either

They will, all of them, mourners, come and go
and mingle and shuffle and stifle smiles
until their awkwardness feels as though
it has crusted around their mouths
and up their faces across their cheeks

They are all the individuals whose phones had
wrung;
whose mailboxes received small cards,

who'd read the lines his daughter wrote

to the obituary editor in last week's gazette,

or endured the Sunday sermon aside

when the preacher – then, as-yet-unacquainted,

paused for a moment to offer sympathies

on behalf of God and those in attendance

Thus, each one present might recall the man,

or prevaricate a special recollected day –

and though the liars ought not be excused

they will extol better with their blasphemy,

speaking as if they'd been granted a peek

at God's own notes in his judgment diary –

> *"You know, heaven just needed one more*
> *good man"*
> *or "he sings with the angels now"*
> *and so, what is the point?*

It doesn't matter – hell or no –

they will all be compelled to compromise

to massage their memories and personal reflections

because memorials are not for the cold and gone

they're for harmonizing with the here and now –

experiences; photos; humorous anecdotes

chestnuts of chagrin; chance turned into fable

the cocks and the bulls; all the fish that got away,
inflated to the extent each participant is able,
and each account inevitably to star
a different protagonist;
each account featuring the unique human being
known only to that particular speaker

While the deceased – if lucky, far out of reach,
or if present, lying up front – cold, stiff and quiet
unable to clarify, rebut or quash
the inaccuracies as they're volunteered
by a collection of conspicuous strangers

Of course, it's not the dead man's fault
the mourners are obliged to puree their thoughts

a few intense memories rendered to soup
in order that they be shared with a group

But I sicken to imagine the Cuisinarted mush
my few vivid recollections of him might become –
hands on hips, snarling down the alley at pins
refusing to bow to his perfect delivery and spin;
walking the stones from the house to the barn
through spring air ripe with magnolia perfume
the navy tattoo obscured by hair on his chest
the time we glued a cherry bomb to the big hornet
nest –

Not a one of those sitting there solemn in a pew
could possibly have known the man with whom
I witnessed such wonders live and expire;
the memories I save are more than possessions
they are immutable, incommunicable mysteries
magical, biochemical, electro-temporal reactions,
beyond anyone's capability to share
not to be conveyed – one had to be there,
and I cannot permit them to be sanded and
smoothed
rough edges softened, all knots removed
in order they conform to the ladles and spoons
of a gathering's easy digestion

I knew the man –
we weren't the closest of friends

but most of his people knew me as well
though they might not know I was a long-time pal

Most of them might be surprised to learn
I stopped to think of him all the time,
oh, not every day perhaps, but often and regularly
considering we'd had so little one-to-one
for several years, I guess I'd say

The memorial service will be held next week
I will not attend

Moving On

It seems nothing more than reflections
now – isn't that all we have?
can we universalize from what it was
then – as if we might pretend
every lesson learned proves out?
tomorrow – what a crock!

Anyone beyond the median years gets
ontology – natural order from disordering things
and the productivity of younger persons
is – so much more than youthful energy –
it is the blessed rush of narcissism
hurrying – the self-preoccupation
and *will* to ignore everyone else.

Bookshelf

All my Hermann Hesse novels –
all hardcover except for *Knulp* –
are lined up at the same height
as the 2-volume book club set
of the *Complete Works*
of William Shakespeare. All these
occupy one shelf just below
several years of the monthly
Poetry, perfect-bound
with white spines like a row
of clean accomplishments.
It's hard to look at these stacks
and not think how beautiful
they are, collected and unread.

Fixing Meaning

Just fixing things
like part of a car, a leaky faucet,
or maybe a crack in the bathroom tile

or maybe just selling things –
used clothes, new houses, furniture,
adventure travel – like a rafting trip down the Nile

or maybe simply completing tasks –
hanging a painting, arranging the closet,
or possibly purging outdated files –

when a day can be filled
with projects like these – projects
with clear beginnings and ends
it's so much easier to lie down at night
free of the doubt about what it all means.

Nothing Ever Happens

A complicated subject, surviving,
whether gerund or adjective,
say it transitive or otherwise
and there's always something left –
but there's also something missing.

Each of us accepts persisting
in whatever way he can –
way to survive, way to deal,
way to leave or be left behind –
to be missed, or do some missing.

But now there may be a new third way.
I discovered this on my own. I pretend
everything has perished, and nothing
has really gone – sure, it may appear
like a type of denial, but sometimes
it feels like nothing ever happened.

Re: a Painting of a Lighthouse

This painting denies me any retreat
will not permit my return to routine –
observer of lives
secret arbiter of the sins of others –
it ridicules me for my timidity.

The artist notes, *"watercolor on paper"*
and I think, "how appropriate" –
where the sea has turned to venom
we sense the presence of deep trenches
dissecting the ocean's floor –
they start to writhe and coil to strike the sky
stinging and hissing at the surface –
frothy, purulent fangs for stabbing the moon.

The myth of saltwater, sea and sand
arose to seduce the sanity of man –
rope and canvas trade winded arias
impregnating sails over beds of wooden planks
bleached by the salted sleet and rain
and scoured raw beneath the grain –

as we, the more vigilant, recognize
a deeper deception even the artist
did not intend.

The lighthouse
it does not warn us away
it does not alert us to danger –
a vampiric light it beckons romantics
blinking its promise to return us home –
all for its need of splinter and bone.

I feel relief that my comrades are gone
I can rue failed voyages all alone
my mates moved on, lost or dead
far from earshot and pitiable pine –
captain? sailor? awash with dread
errors all, and all of them mine –

No – we were never safe, we misunderstood
we were no more than staid and sound
with footsteps landing on solid ground
when we indulged our earliest innocent dreams –

to look experienced, muscular and manly
scarred by battles with ancient serpents
tattooed with needles of scrimshaw and quartz
twirled in the alleys of exotic ports –

We had dreamt of a world of seven mirrors
pools for our reflecting between the continents –
they would stretch the distance, from deck to
horizon
to kiss the lower lip of a rising full moon –
we would smile from the gunnels, rubbing callouses
we acquired as we polished antique harpoons

We are not adventurers, we are only victims –
victims of our own vision
we see the lighthouse so very clearly
from halfway round the world
before our vessel has left the harbor
before we have even set foot on board –
by the warming hearth in our reading room
in the comfort of bed when we turn out the light –
in our sheltered dreams throughout the night
we see the lighthouse wink its welcome
beguiling us, take heart and leave home

I have sailed, I have captained, and wrecked
upon the rocks, but also sunk into the deep –
this painting sees and accuses me,
understands and refuses me any retreat.

Mutual Loss

For several days after, we did not talk.
You needed to, but I've always hated
the idea that talking offers comfort.
Then, when the silence grew too deep
you began expressing anger about heirlooms –
antique chairs, a painting –
with no response from *dead's* end.

I could feel your incredulity.
You pictured all of us decades ago,
seated around the annual Christmas tree,
each year decked-out and gouging its own
scratches in the family room ceiling
with the point of that gaudy ornamental star –
or you might have been recalling the year
dad hired that portrait photographer
(*the leprechaun with the toupee?*) who
arranged the entire family –
nuclear and extended –
according to height, presciently dividing

soon-to-be-separated spouses, and flinging
soon-to-leave-home teens across the world
to the far end of the big couch.

And you can't help thinking, albeit destined
to be divided due to all the unpredictables,
we were so together back then.
The thing is, for all we know he might
be remembering all of that, too –
and like me, doing his best to not dwell.

I stand in my kitchen beneath a still life print –
perhaps it imitates a famous oil.
I never checked. It fits its frame –
do you recall it hanging in the dining room
at grandma's house?
And a question never stops scratching
at the ceiling of my mind –
more pointed than any Christmas tree star –
is there an uncle or an aunt somewhere
wondering what became of that picture,
and cursing the loss that orphaned it?

So I won't lament the orphaned things –
will not indulge our missing her –
like old antiques and paintings, her being
here never belonged to us –
all of it is mutual loss.

She Was Fine

When I visited my sister in the hospital –
near the beginning of the end,
when it was already understood
she would likely get up and walk around,
enjoy food and laughter with friends
and visitors, but she was not going
to go back home –
I stood at the end of her bed,
marveling at the high-tech mechanics
and adjustable controllers,
watching her elevate her upper torso
while, at the same time, she turned
the sound down on the wall-mounted TV.
She was smiling the whole time.
I asked how she was doing –
like, "how-ya doin'?" –
and she must have noticed a hint
of uncharacteristically serious concern
leaking through my normal irreverence,
because her response sounded like
an attempt to ease someone's mind –
she smiled and laughed, and said, "I'm fine."

I think back now –
what else would you say?
It was only thirty days later she was gone –
straight from hospital to hospice, and then on.

Dying may always be a permanent thing,
but sometimes it's too abrupt –
it ought to mean something more than a moment,
but that was the last lesson my sister taught me –
she was fine, and then she was gone.

What Gets Me

What gets me is we act hurt,
as if it's a surprise –
we're caught off guard –
no one alerted us to this possibility.
Someone (a loved one) takes ill,
terminally ill, and dies –
maybe it's mom, or dad, or a sister,
but those of us who write poems
start expressing our dismay in verse –
empty houses, routines of comfort –
gone, like, all-of-a-sudden,
souls passed on.

Elephants grieve the loss of family –
so do wolves and parrots,
but they did not take biology
in high school.

I've heard a macho stereotype expressed –
a deathbed rant –
a limp-muscled, scruffy-bearded
old barstool claim-jumper,
shaking his fist at the ceiling –
imagining God to be up there somewhere

just beyond the acoustical tiles

and fluorescent bulbs –

screaming for a fair shot,

"Me and two good men could

whip this thing!"

The Principle

We might have tried astronomy
or theoretical physics –
you know, cosmological studies –
those fields where we meet the beginning
when the gullet of the universe
gathered in its very first gulp.

We have always been fascinated
by those questions –
all those "why's" and "how's" –
where did we come from?
why are we here?
and where are we going to wind up?

But we were also drawn to poetry,
and the strictly philosophical –
like, why is there always a "why" anyhow –
and after years of trying and failing
we arrived at the recognition,
expansion of the question may never stop.

Separation moved us to communicate
despite our differing diction –
gluons, quarks, bosons, the Higgs –
in the druidic symbols of Einstein and Newton,
and which they could readily distinguish
as well as we, a bottom from its top.

When we noted that a rhyme scheme
might permeate the entire cosmos –
perhaps even a meter for all existence –
few in the lab treated it as apropos,
arguing the notion just made no sense.
So we hypothesized that a plumb bob, dropped

into any line in any poem,
intended to make a true determination –
to accurately critique the verse in motion –
would always prove we can't measure both,
where we are, and where we are going . . .
because a poem might well be just a wave,
but it's also just ink on pulp.

Comparability

We were promised something special –
we were told it would be grand,
and we expected to be awed
by the scope of its grandeur,
but it was less – not bad, but "un"

When it was over we worried
    which link was missing?
    was it message?
    the messenger's tone?
    had we forgotten how to listen?

Then somebody commented the story
was too particular to be grand
and we realized it was.

We had been hoping for a bigger notion –
a thought we could compare,
but no one knew his wife
or understood her moods, or cared
    about the way she looked at the moon
    or left scraps for the birds and squirrels
    or nurtured wild flowers
    at the edge of the forest.

Then the fire cracked and spat,
and a fox that had been lying near the edge
of our circle – just beyond the light –
spoke up and said,
"glories ought to be saved for the glorious,"
and he turned and walked into
the deeper darkness
and we all nodded in agreement.

Why Poets Like Flowers

So, we'll admit poets love birds and flowers –
no, that's not exactly right. Poets love
wine, whiskey, opium and speed –
and then, once they get their biochemistry set
they can't help recognizing the beauty
and meaning in everything else –
especially colorful things which never
intended to be so showy.

What Song Is This

I might ask myself, am I a poor listener?
Cursed with an untrained ear?
Is it my brain? or my upbringing?
or the upbringing of my brain?

I've tried, more than once, to walk
out on the lawn at dawn and listen
to the birds singing, and hear a prayer
in their chorus. I'm sorry. I don't hear it.

First, yes, I hear birds, and I assume
I am hearing the same song
others have heard at such times,
in such circumstances. And I also hear
the morning's first bees buzz-bombing,
flower to flower over the clover
still damp with dew –
plus there's the hum of early commuters
on the freeway a half-mile south,
and from high above the intermittent,
muffled whinge of the turbofans of 737s
lining up for their turns to land at Hartsfield.

It's early, but a couple of lawn services
have already fired up their gas-powered
mowers and blowers in the neighborhood.
They may get a few extra yards in before
day's end, or at least beat some of its heat.

These sounds, and dozens of others
(perhaps hundreds) to which I've
become so inured I no longer distinguish
them, no longer recognize their presence,
soak the spot where I stand. And if I
move in any direction, regardless
of my pace, the immersive symphony
moves with me. No velocity will
deliver escape.

If I stand still and concentrate I can
return, all the way back to the first bird
of the morning. I think it's a Robin, but it
might be a Carolina Wren, and it
doesn't matter because it's too hard
to put that much focus into moments
so inconsequential – the first fifteen
or twenty minutes of any day –
when I'm not yet fully awake, and

when there's no way I will ever figure
out, or care, who's singing what song.

Anatomy of the Process

First, recognize that motivation
is the fuel of will –
sometimes wholly drilled and refined inside,
sometimes shipped in and arriving from outside –
combusted to accomplish a task –

Where "task" is any by-the-numbers job –
small (pick up your room)
large (fix the roof before winter),
important (fix the roof before winter)
or inconsequential (pick up your room) –

However, inspiration is a special kind of fuel –
high performance and distinguished
from other kinds of combustible motivation
for its unique suitability to creation –

creation being that task-like function –
done for process as opposed to result.

One Surface

As a group we approach the water's edge,
its shimmer pulling us forward
to the very lick and spray of wetness
silver splinters of light skip and glitter
calling each of us by name.

Each of us will scan the horizon
each of us seeing a separate distance
though always in miniature –
inverting, stretching, warping –
across billions of tiny ripples.

Some would elect to wade right in
convinced of a shallow safety
and its invitation to all –
others anticipate depth and danger
and make themselves ready
for greater angst and peril.

Alternately scared, then disappointed,
those who sought the deeper waters
are lost in fathoms or eaten by monsters –
while the waders remain safe
albeit unanointed –

and gazes fixed sternly at the surface
they only imagine threats of the deep.

Outcomes

Do I enjoy these syllables?
Do they sneak in through my
pupils to my mind, or do
they bounce off the outside
of my head, repelled by sideburns,
earlobes and piercings?
Do they penetrate to gray neurons,
and go sliding up and down
the tubes and chutes of my thoughts?

The birthing hurts, I can tell you that much.
The canal is too tight for weighty things,
and there is never enough placenta
for a truly healthy parturition.

A new father, expecting to see
a grateful smile, all wet and cooing,
meets only screams of agony –
accusations for this, and everything he's done.
They lie there, bloodying the clean white sheets

of the tables and desks in delivery rooms –
opening their gummy eyelids, they shout,
"why in the world did you let me out?"

Nothing New

It's all colorful birds and flowers,
or maybe insects – like butterflies
and bumblebees. Even the gloom is
colorful because gray is never
just ugly gray.

Then there's night – not just dark
night, but black, and with dots
of sugar crystals pretending
to be stars.

Then come confessions – one's
broken heart, or another for having
broken a heart. And on it goes –
an industrial system generating
lines for a universe that has never
known colorblindness.

Not Talking

It's hard to not say –
easy to say briefly
but difficult to convey.

I hate this –
having minds separate
unable to connect.
I will do exactly everything
I can do –
if you cannot hear me
then I'm not talking to you.

In

The first 16 pages are stoic grays
perforated with bullet holes of shiny
black and white – and then,
off-centered, at least east and west,
perhaps also north and south,
splashes of carmine and cyan,
and a stripe of mustard surrounding
the faces of several zombies
with a couple of vampires
in their midst – as if they'd always
put up with each other.

Sometimes there's one page
bled beyond the edge with a picture
of an emerald forest, and
in the center of the leaves and limbs,
dripping bits of gooey black rot,
and adorned with jeweled bracelets –
the slick trails of snails –

stands an albinic Cinderella
in white veil and gown –
as bright as any studio klieg,
her rose red lips pursed to frown.

Tracklayers

I recall my time among the tracklayers,

side-by-side with competitors and friends

we roared into the emptiness,
piloting our separate trains –

with sweat from brows burning our eyes,

we glared our anger at the open space,

our muscles torn by hammer swings –

not one old tie left spiked in place –

inventor - risk-taker – entrepreneur,

inebriated of sobriquets,

we dreamt of wings and tossing rails,

denying a world of measures and weights –

gravity suspended - our reason floated

to dreams of conquests yet to be,

addicted to notions of life forever

ours for the taking - by sheer tenacity

we blistered our skin with faster speeds

we died discretely - but all together

battling the universe - attempting to will

the fix of spikes driven in ether.

Tilted Memory

for a Sunday afternoon, ca. 1972,
at Sam's Anchor Café in Tiburon

Back when it was just a dockside bar,
before George Lucas bought the Presidio,
Sam's had an antique pinball machine
which knew me too well and
would tell my secrets to anyone
with a quarter.

I would start out strong, rising,
elevating toward achievements unnumbered.
When I rounded my first arc
I could feel success within reach.
They tried their best to block me –
to slam me from both sides, by surprise,
with rebounding energies
mysteriously enhanced,
electrically, mechanically.
I always discovered new avenues
of escape, and should those fail
I would nearly always evade their stops.

True, I died –

on occasion I was forced to resurrect

myself, perhaps again and again,

but I would amass millions

prior to any resignation,

and that would be only temporary –

for minutes, for another glass

of Grenache Rosé, perhaps a retreat

until next Sunday afternoon –

but only temporary.

If the old memory hurts, it's only because

the passing of time has clarified

the scope of my losses –

always bumping into strangers,

using them for what I could,

characterizing them as partnerships

on my way down –

then looking back up and

forever trying to replay the path

in my mind, for more millions,

destined to a certain death –

though only temporary.

Three Ironies of Regret

Every once in a while – maybe every other day
I recall some regrettable past circumstance

maybe I was sixteen – maybe I was twenty-three
it doesn't matter since it was so long ago

but, do I see a witness? another human on the scene
whose audience can catalyze the pierce of
recollected shame?

And that's the first irony – that memories lose
sharpness
while their points remain keen enough to cut,

so I'm usually already bleeding by the time I stop
to reflect on the second irony – the witness I recall

is not behaving with shock and revulsion – as I now
imagine my action to have evoked in everyone,

thus, the second irony – the witness I remember
failed to recognize my sin – saw me being comedic
or clever

and then the third irony catches up to my consciousness –

that the witness – no matter how acute his comprehension

nor how confused – can no longer inspire a reverie of shame.

He has been dead for years – then this third irony triggers

a subtle tickle to the mind – of all my shameful memories

perhaps none merits regret – only the self-indulgence of my

recollections earns ignominy now – and we surely can't trust him

or there would never have been an original sin to recall.

Real Me

If I step out of my front door
to stand on the front porch,
or more, if I step out onto the front walk,
or further, if I leave the walk
and step over to the border
of the front garden where
bouquets of azaleas shoot color
into the air like young delinquents
with Super Soaker guns,
then I become a Kooser or an Oliver –
but if I stay inside looking at my desk,
or allow my eyes to wander
over the spines of books on my shelves,
or even if I haven't come that far,
and I'm still standing, spitting and blinking
beneath the hot water of my morning shower,
then I am more a Hesse or a Sartre.

I ought to be grateful to possess some power
over the programming of my person,

but perhaps I should be ashamed

there may be so little *real me* –

that where I stand will complete this composition.

The Egotist

The egotist does not rue the loss
of loved ones for what he never
got round to saying –
he believes he said everything
that needed to be said.
He wishes he could bring them back –
perhaps a mother, a father, a sister –
if only for a moment,
not to tell them something
he never told them,
but to tell them something
he probably told them more than once –
to tell them again
so they'll never forget.

When the Lake Freezes

Geese and ducks sweating their auditions,
rehearse for the toughest roles they play –
dramatic gazes to a far horizon,
or less distant point across the lake,
pretending the season has spatial boundary
an edge where warmer air awaits.

Waddles betray the stilted caution –
peccant tiptoes of webbed keratin
placed fainter than the fall of shedding down
as if pressed to a bed of knife tips and pins –
a susurrant slap of feathers to flank,
and each bill curls to a painful grin.

The stage is strewn with plant debris –
leaves and limbs from shrubs and trees,
desiccated by dehydrating breath
of January – scarred, scabbed and broken
from beating themselves on the frozen floor.
All dead on water – all died of thirst,
while a few of them even deeper cursed,
having discovered the diviner's quest
one end soaked and marking access
the other end lofted skyward, askew –

a coat of silver, and hoarfrost has wrought
winter's glory to the blackened rot.

Tinnitus

More like a hissing of the sizzling air
than a variant of scale or tone,
the conflagration starts up again,
and again and again each dawn –
      incinerating all the beauty,
      and with it all the calm –
      making ash of all those summer lawns.

Stiff yet filmy, like skins of snakes,
morning breezes sting the head –
membranes recoil, the cochlea aches
at the shriek of nature's dread –
      from far off now come rending sounds,
      as a blue-green planet gets ripped to shreds.

A dissonant rumble approaches and tongues,
and fondles a squalid plain –
with a greasy, pyroclastic kiss,
it bequeaths a charnel stain –
      while roars of blowers and power mowers
      grate against our grain.

Were we deaf to the siren's irony –
now she threatens as she once seduced,

as alarms in shops and homes and cars
rupture more vital and deeper tissues –

      these are not the songs of life,

      but the throes of death turned up – let loose.

Do we sense immersion in the wailing and cries –
the sound of our grasping – gasping for breath?
Swept up in tsunami, we flail for Eden,
convinced the filth of that frothy crest

      disguises a potion for our permanent health,

      all the while our tickets bear the bright
      shibboleth –

      this ride will undoubtedly end with our
      death.

Now the sky's become a giant tympanum –
gelled smoke and soot from a century of sin,
the air now hums as the desert might sing –
we dance to the sound of our favorite poison –

      and while the volumes rise, no one will act

      save an involuntary flinch to protect his
      skin.

Accustomed, as we are, to our own suffocation,
we asphyxiate, tapping to the beat of our bliss –
and tone deaf, now, to a planet's screams,

suitably quelled to a background hiss –
  we accepted inertia as immutable law,
  and took comfort with the growing tinnitus.

Skyscraper

It doesn't help when I stop
and reflect on the fact
such monsters are designed
and built by mortals –
they might rise by the will
of architects, the calculations
of engineers –
blueprints and blue pens –
but they snarl in the dark,
with their exhaust fans
as big as dump trucks
and humpbacked turbines
the size of jumbo jets –
wires, tunnels, grease and steam.

Watch those bulbous feeders
roll in, their bloated bellies extended,
churning volumes of gray vomit
to pour over frames and rebar.

Go below where the innards echo,
and the stomach hisses with
undigested mephitis, readying
the release of its engorging gasses.

The skyscraper puts on a pretty face,
but underneath it is all nightmare –
stacked high under puttied glass, threaded
together with shafts and ductwork.

His Lake

They stroll the path weaving their way,
lives laced tight by arm and eyelet,
bound by commitment and communal debt –
some prior glories now turned to regret,
while they avoid the panorama of the Heron's lake.
The water invites, but it's not for their sake.

The turtles – river Cooters – Malian refugees
rest piggyback above the rocks and logs.
The banded water snakes will find the sun,
then wait in ambush for their bugs and frogs,
as the cloudless noon sky continues to bake
the banks of cracked mud around the lake.

The dragonflies darting just two steps ahead
feign preoccupation, like we won't notice
their precision so we might well forget
a flight so exact bespeaks great purpose.
And droplet-jeweled ducks inflate and shake,
then turn topsy-turvy head down in the lake.

At the edge of this lake his majesty struts,
then freezes to study a shallow of reeds.
His mastery of stealth and nonchalance
lulls the little things upon which he feeds.
He shares the water with the brant goose and drake,
but everyone knows that this is his lake.

Get The Idea

I get it. I understand how brothers
wore different uniforms and killed
each other in the Civil War –
and I don't need a description
of the circumstances in Israel, or Gaza,
or Syria – anywhere, today, yesterday,
a hundred years ago – to imagine
how it happens again and again.
Blood counts. It's thick. But ideas
are combustible. I would have looked
down that barrel, across the field
and seen my brother wearing Gray,
and I would have thought –
"Are you kidding me? Do you
think I'm going to let someone
from my family live that stupid?"

You Can See The Wires

If your vision is good –
not necessarily 20/20,
but better is better –
and the air is clear and clean
so that particulate pollution is low,
and you are looking at the world
within in a single medium
so that refraction does not contribute
to distortion of the visual image, then
if you stand very still and
take a moment to concentrate
you can see the wires –
your wires, my wires, the wires
that move our cars and planes –
the wires that hold us in place.

For me, the problem was not
the recognition that we may be puppets,
but recognizing the production
was too low-budget
to make us look more real.

Uncertainty

Is it the saddest time of a life
when a person stops asking,
stops thinking –
when opinions harden to certainty,
not because he is certain –
not for evidence and proof,
but because he is overtaken by fear –
afraid of learning he was wrong all along.

Why Cosmologists Stay Young

"Kids are never the problem. They are born
scientists.

      The problem is always the adults."

              Neil deGrasse Tyson

When we were young we pursued

truth relentlessly –

unless we met up with classmates,

when we would be forced to act

more confident about things

we had no way of knowing –

we were not liars, but we were young males,

and under the right conditions

testosterone tends to push

the immature male to assert confidence

regarding nearly everything,

no matter how uncertain.

But then, the pursuit of truth requires youth.

It does not require young age, but youth

is different. Pursuing truth requires

the ability to admit wrong –

wrong directions, incorrect assumptions

regarding prior theories recently held.

We are not sure why aging seems
to most often limit, even eliminate,
those options, particularly for males.
Perhaps older men feel responsible
for knowing more, and thus they
are pushed to sound as if they are
always surrounded by classmates –
even when many are already dead.
Perhaps it's because older men
often feel responsible for other lives,
and they wish to sound knowledgeable
and authoritative in order to lend
a measure of confidence to progeny.

This is why, we now believe, cosmologists
tend to remain youthful (if not young).
They are constantly pursuing truth, and
continuously reminded of how wrong
they were recently.

Seriously

Sometimes I *think* the most amazing things,
and sometimes I even do them –
but most of the time I don't do them,
even the most amazing things, seriously.
I think to myself, this is amazing, or
it would be amazing if I were serious,
but there will be time for that later
when I'm more serious more often.
Then I look at something I was thinking
and doing back before I got serious
and I realize it was more amazing
than what I am doing in all seriousness.
But then I also realize that had I tried
to do that thing seriously back then,
I would probably have worn myself out
being serious, and would have had nothing
left to get me this far.

And so, once there were amazing but
not serious things, and now there seem

to be a lot of serious things
of minimal amazement.

And I'm still not sure why.

Objects of Objectives

They set out, eyes to one horizon,
perhaps a focus on one particular thing –
was it a tree? rocks? a shadow?
from that distance they could not be certain,

but the ambiguity was exciting –
until they were moved to make a decision.
It was a giant cauldron cast of gold
(explaining the occasional glint when the sky
blinked and the sun shone through the overcast).

Callouses, cuts, broken bones –
the insults of an envious world
scarred their bodies without mercy.
The universe would always be jealous
of their energy, and even more, their naiveté –
that combustible mixture, immaturity and youth,
enabling them to go for broke, fail,
and go broke multiple times per day.

They were not deterred. They grabbed a granola bar
and drank a Mountain Dew, and just kept moving –
kept on exerting, and dreaming –
and finally they ended up at the edge, discovering

that most of the warnings had been legit.
Still, the effort wasn't wasted.

This was the point where they learned the lesson –
the lesson of the lemons and lemonade –
of course the fruit is acidic and tart,
but they were young and foolish and thirsty –
and swore their facial pucker and wince
was simply the result of travails so sweet.

That Lamp

There appears to be some confusion regarding
the search for truth and honesty these days.

I blame Diogenes, that tetchy ancient Turk
who greeted everyone the same –
saint, sinner, statesman –
like they were all pitchmen hawking
miracle cleaning formulas on late night TV.

It's become difficult to raise a lamp –
even to light a match –
close to a person's face
to confirm his integrity.

And so, those of us who have
long sought truth only to discover
honor absent among our fellows,
have deferred to the suspicion
everyone is lying. They call us "cynics."

We were looking for honesty,
not denying its potential –
but it's very difficult these days
to keep that lamp lit.

Real Easy

When we really study a subject –
like a subject fit for serious pursuit –
we find it to be more complex than
we might have initially imagined.
Like when we meet a really good
racquetball player (a club pro maybe),
or someone who really knows how
to keep a garden and produce tasty
vegetables and watermelons, and
pumpkins in October (a green thumb),
we sometimes think to ourselves,
"Hey, I could do that." And then,
when we begin pursuing that activity,
and we start to learn all the things
that can go wrong, and all the mistakes
one must learn to avoid, or learn
to redress in order to be good
at that pursuit –
not to mention the many degrees
of practiced, good, better, *improved,*
excellent and *champion* we discover we
must traverse (just as the really
accomplished model we initially
witnessed must have done) in order

to achieve the level of proficiency
which first inspired us. It always
looks so much easier than it really is.

The Leak of Ideas

They leak, don't they?
Ideas leak –
right out of the brain because
there is no good spigot
to control that flow.

They drip out of eyes and ears.
They spew from mouths,
out onto the floor to puddle
on carpets, or run like dog urine
over the hardwoods
to the first crack they find.

You can't mop them up.
They aren't like spilt milk
or the coffee that dribbles from cups
you thought were empty when
you loaded the dishwasher –
no, it requires forethought
so when the leaking starts
you can use a pen or pencil –
something that can sponge them
onto the pages of a notebook, or
perhaps, if one is extraordinarily adept,

catch them in mid-fall
with a sound recording device.

The real trouble with leaking ideas
is they often just look like waste –
dirty water, soap suds, cold soup –
until they've fully escaped.
Then, all of a sudden you
realize what's got away.
I hate that.

Burning Question

The good questions do not come stabbing
like clean arrows into the mind.
They may float down like falling leaves –
often an inspiring vision.

Occasionally, they seep in through your feet
the way melting snow in the gutter
will do with your shoes –
the icy slush is dirty, but appears firm,
then you step from the curb
and you're soaked with the question.

Now its penetrated. If it's meaningless
it will likely mildew and discolor. By the time
you get to it you will have to bleach it out
completely – no amount of cleansing will
get it clean enough to consider and answer.

If it's meaningful, it may turn philosophical,
and that means it will likely ferment.
The danger here being the fermentation
which, by itself, provides a certain sustenance.
Such questions are often intoxicating,
and sometimes even addictive.

I burn mine.

I light them on fire and watch as they engulf
themselves, fueled by their own theoretical yeast.
They burn very warm with a warmth that
can be shared, and that's not even the most
beautiful part. The really beautiful part
is the poem which results.

A poem is always in the ash of a philosophical fire.

Section II

After Shopping for Happiness

A Gift of Happiness

When the new **MegaMetaStore**
opened outside of town,
the lines went from the door
all the way out through the parking lot –
across the highway,
across the fields,
and into the next county.

At least that's as far as the news media
observed and reported –
so who knows for sure?!

It was days before I procured a cart
inside and began perusing the aisles.
That was a Monday but I felt
fortunate for getting in while the store
was still celebrating its Grand Opening –
the whole place was crazy,
all I could think was,
"if this is a typical **MMS** shopping
experience, then I don't want to be
around for the holidays!"

As one might expect, the *Meaning of Life*
department was packed with shoppers
of every type and walk of life –
indigents shopping alongside CEOs,
bankers and lawyers –
the Salvation Army-clad elbow-to-elbow
with tailored suits, and
the majority clustering around
end-aisle promotional displays,
featuring the latest how-to products
from Parker Brothers and Nintendo.

It only occurred to me later, but
there were no moms in *Meaning* –
well, what I mean to say is most
of the customers who looked like moms
were not to be found in that department –
in fact, they were filling the aisles,
bumping each other's strollers and baby
carriers over in *Health and Legacy.*

By contrast (for those who note such trends),
the dads were nowhere near the moms –
indeed, most of them were as far
from *Health and Legacy* as the store

layout permitted –

over with the younger guys and college kids,

going item-by-item in the section

marked *Masculinity*, where the rows

were filled with a variety

of priapean products designed to appeal

to every imaginable post-puberty

niche of man and boy –

sub-sections categorized by interactive

SKU-specific signage –

labels like: *Virility, Authority, Control* and *Cars*.

One large section, *Attributes*, was identified

by a giant mobile suspended from the ceiling.

It was bright and colorful from a distance,

so I walked a few of those aisles to get

a sense of what was there –

it turned out to be minor apps

and personality plug-ins like,

Generosity, Loyalty, Honesty, and so on.

No sales assistant was present,

and by comparison with the rest

of the store, *Attributes* looked to be

on more of a self-serve system –

indeed, some aspects of appearance,

such as *Complexion* and *IQ Upgrades*,
were only available via vending machines.
The section was nearly empty of shoppers,
and I figured that, like me, most people
felt they already had things to fill
those needs and spaces at home.

That said, while I was skimming the items
in *Attributes*, the idea of *Love* came to mind –
it seemed to fit with *Loyalty*, *Commitment*
and some of the other products advertised –
in hindsight, I might have surmised the answer,
(even if I couldn't intuit the rationale) –
Love is a big enough category to support
its own branded section.

And so, curiosity moved me to check
out the *Love* department –
(by the way, *Curiosity* was also available
back in *Attributes*, but I already felt well-stocked).
I must say the merchandising strategy in *Love*
struck me as very confusing –
every aisle and arch into *Love* featured
a freestanding floor sign:

"Note: *Love* is not a self-serve department –
for *Desire*, *Attractiveness*, *Wooability*,
and other Lust-related products, please
visit aisles in the *Attributes* department."

I did not spend much time in *Love* –
it felt ominous by comparison
to other sections, and though
it was busy with other shoppers,
including a surprising number of children,
I did not see anything I felt I needed
at the moment.

If I had a specific purchase objective
that day, it would be in *Happiness* –
I was not looking for anything big –
nothing with a lifetime guarantee,
not even a year's supply –
a simple lagniappe to inspire the day,
perhaps a token good for a week's worth –
maybe even something I could use as a gift.
Then, yes, I was able to use such a
relatively defined shopping errand as my
excuse to get a handle on this store.

See, it was my initial intent to locate
Happiness which led me to *Meaning*
in the first place,
but then I'd gotten sidetracked –
so now, winding my way back
I noticed a large placard with an arrow
pointing to a separate room for *Religion* –
it was just off the *Meaning of Life* section.

I couldn't help it. I had to go check that out!

A wide, well-lit alcove connected the
Religion department with the rest of the store,
but at the same time, gave one the impression
of entering a completely different
space and place –
and upon entering the alcove
shoppers were greeted by another
freestanding floor sign:

"Note: you are entering *Religion*,
featuring items of *Rite, Ceremony, Custom,
Apparel, Interior Design, Money, Weapons*
and *War* – for *Piety, Devotion* and
other *Faith*-related items, please

visit aisles in the *Attributes* department."

It turned out to be a real hassle
because I didn't notice the alcove
to *Religion* was one-way –
most of the customers did not seem
all that distressed by the fact
there was no obvious way of getting back
to the main store –
once I was inside it quickly became
obvious there would be very few items
to interest me, but I was stuck –
at least until I could find an exit, so
I did my best to get a sense of the stuff
on display, and make this visit count.

I can't really estimate the room's dimensions –
to begin with, it was pretty dark,
and difficult for the eyes to adjust –
but, generally speaking, the room
appeared quite long,
while at the same time extremely narrow,
with terrible acoustics –
walls of echo and distortion drenching
everyone from vaulted ceilings.

A couple of Christians were browsing
a table of remainders
in the center of the room.

A huddle of bearded Muslim dudes,
in hijabs and kufis, occupied
a prominent corner,
while next to them a large group
of Hasidim eyed some inventory
with classic lines –
though they seemed annoyed by a posse
of young Mizrahi and Sephardim,
texting and Tweeting between themselves
regarding the latest fashions.

On the other side of the narrow space
a straggle of Buddhists and Hindus
shopped shelves of modernist designs –
they stood close together, carefully fingering
a select few products with simple clean lines
and muted colors, but they went out of their way
to avoid any person-to-person contact –
not a one of them made a purchase,
as far as I could tell, but everybody

was smiling and seemed generally happy
with the day's marketing experience.

As I ventured further into the room
I came upon additional customers –
some shopping solo – some as couples,
or in small cliques of close friends
with shared perspective and taste.

Sub-sections were not marked very clearly
and one could easily drift from, say,
shelves of Jewish or Christian products
over into the items intended for Pagans and
Witches without even noticing –
but everyone appeared to be envious
of the items of interior décor –
everything from candles and tablecloths,
to drapes and towels –
on the shelves laid out for worshippers
of the Moon and Sun.

In spite of the appeal of the Pagan fabric prints,
the best lamps and electrical appliances
were found over by the UFO religion displays –
the flying saucer sconces and lanterns, and

the L. Ron Hubbard microwaves would have made
fantastic additions to anyone's home.

I'd say I bounced around in *Religion*
for at least an hour or more, when I came
to a sign that just read, "tixe" taped next
to a sliding door –
it was glass, but I couldn't see through,
it could have been a prop –
where shoppers were supposed to slide it open
and find that it led nowhere, but as soon as I
started to pull the handle the door slid an inch
or two, pulling the taped sign back to reveal
"exit" handwritten on a poster –

it had been posted, accidentally upside down,
and sure enough, sunlight came streaming in
and lit one whole end of the room.

I stepped outside through a turnstile gate
a numbered card popped up –
it said I was the six hundred and sixty-sixth
consumer de-programmed that day –
and in smaller print it promised if I returned
within the month and applied for an
MMS credit card, then I would be entitled to
any number of heavenly rewards.
From that spot a series of chevrons, brightly
painted on the floor guided me back
to the front of the store where anyone
possessed of a turnstile card could cut the lines
and walk right in the huge front door.

Now, by that time I was all shopped-out –
tired of browsing and being on my feet –
but the **MegaMetaStore** has no food court
where you can grab a bite to eat. Still,
I wasn't about to waste a day without
so much as one peek at *Happiness* –
perhaps even find a bargain

on that special little thing –

that small token I would recognize when I saw it –

like, it would call out from its shelf

and tell me it was the thing

I'd been looking for.

No wonder I missed it the first time around,

Happiness turned out to be

the smallest of all the departments –

lucky for me, most things in *Happiness*

were appropriately sized and priced –

many were tiny and relatively cheap,

and all the more so for the grand opening.

Shelves held a wide range of bobbles

and favors and gifty-type things,

everything colorfully boxed –

and while I never got that, "this is it!"

feeling about any particular item,

I picked out one little token which

fit my pocket very nicely –

then, just as I was readying to head

back to the register

I caught sight of yet another
of those freestanding signs:

"Note: due to State Blue Rules,
items in the *Happiness* department
may not be purchased on Mondays."

"For shit's sake," I mumbled to myself,
"how idiotic is that?!"

I'd spent weeks trying to get inside this place
to find one little bit of happiness –
I finally gained access to learn
I could purchase any idea –
any philosophy or mood without consequence,
without any conscience or care –
but I was twenty-four hours out of synch
to buy one little happy notion.

I drove home feeling dirty –
as if I'd applied for a position and been told
I was not qualified for the job –
like I'd betrayed some unwritten
teleological mercantile code of the universe –
like the one that keeps dimensions five through 11

from bumping into height, width and depth –
the one that governs the delicate balance
of inventories and needs –
in other words, life and death.

The **MegaMetaStore** fliers tout
among the big box's marketing roles
is not just providing for humanity's dreams,
but maintenance and upkeep on our rented souls.
Yes, the place was new and big and clean –
you have to give some credit to them,
but as far as enjoyable shopping goes,
next time I'll order direct from Amazon.